MY SOFTBALL STATS

COPYRIGHT 2015
PRESTO~BRANDO PUBLISHING

MY SPORTS STATS BOOKS ~ BY: KIM KATT

Season _____ Year _____ My Age _____

ME

A
N
D

MY TEAM NAME :

MY TEAM

MY COACHES:

_____

_____

MY TEAM:

1. _____   2. _____

3. _____   4. _____

5. _____   6. _____

7. _____   8. _____

9. _____   10. _____

11. _____   12. _____

13. _____   14. _____

15. _____   16. _____

MY TEAM COLORS: _____

MY JERSEY SIZE: _____

MY JERSEY NUMBER: _____

MY CLEATS SIZE: _____

MY FAVORITE ATHLETE:

_____

MY FAVORITE SPORTS TEAM:

_____

MY FAVORITE SPORTS MOVIE:

_____

MY FAVORITE SOFTBALL POSITION:

_____

MY FAVORITE MOTTO:

_____

GAME 1

DATE: _____

WE PLAYED AGAINST: _____

INNINGS I PLAYED: _____ POSITIONS I PLAYED: _____

FIELD I PLAYED ON: _____ POSITION I BATTED_____

ON OFFENSE I HAD:

_____ HITS _____ WALKS _____ HIT BY PITCHES

_____ SINGLES _____ DOUBLES _____ TRIPLES

_____ HOMERUNS _____ GRANDSLAMS _____ RBI'S

_____ STOLEN BASES _____ OUTS _____ STRIKEOUTS

ON DEFENSE I HAD:

_____ CATCHES _____ DOUBLE PLAYS _____ ERRORS

_____ OUTS _____ GROUNDERS _____ POPFLIES

PITCHES:

_____ K'S _____ WALKS _____ HIT BATTER

_____ BALLS _____ STRIKES _____ TOTAL PITCHES

_____ WON _____ LOST _____ TIED _____ SCORE

GAME 2

DATE: _____

WE PLAYED AGAINST: _____

INNINGS I PLAYED: _____ POSITIONS I PLAYED: _____

FIELD I PLAYED ON: _____ POSITION I BATTED_____

ON OFFENSE I HAD:

_____ HITS _____ WALKS _____ HIT BY PITCHES

_____ SINGLES _____ DOUBLES _____ TRIPLES

_____ HOMERUNS _____ GRANDSLAMS _____ RBI'S

_____ STOLEN BASES _____ OUTS _____ STRIKEOUTS

ON DEFENSE I HAD:

_____ CATCHES _____ DOUBLE PLAYS _____ ERRORS

_____ OUTS _____GROUNDERS _____POPFLIES

PITCHES:

_____ K'S _____ WALKS _____ HIT BATTER

_____ BALLS _____ STRIKES _____ TOTAL PITCHES

_____WON _____LOST _____TIED _____ SCORE

GAME 3

DATE: _____

WE PLAYED AGAINST: _____

INNINGS I PLAYED: _____ POSITIONS I PLAYED: _____

FIELD I PLAYED ON: _____ POSITION I BATTED_____

ON OFFENSE I HAD:

_____ HITS _____ WALKS _____ HIT BY PITCHES

_____ SINGLES _____ DOUBLES _____ TRIPLES

_____ HOMERUNS _____ GRANDSLAMS _____ RBI'S

_____ STOLEN BASES _____ OUTS _____ STRIKEOUTS

ON DEFENSE I HAD:

_____ CATCHES _____ DOUBLE PLAYS _____ ERRORS

_____ OUTS _____GROUNDERS _____POPFLIES

PITCHES:

_____ K'S _____ WALKS _____ HIT BATTER

_____ BALLS _____ STRIKES _____ TOTAL PITCHES

_____WON _____LOST _____TIED _____ SCORE

PHOTOS:

GAME 4

DATE: _____

WE PLAYED AGAINST: _____

INNINGS I PLAYED: _____ POSITIONS I PLAYED: _____

FIELD I PLAYED ON: _____ POSITION I BATTED_____

ON OFFENSE I HAD:

_____ HITS _____ WALKS _____ HIT BY PITCHES

_____ SINGLES _____ DOUBLES _____ TRIPLES

_____ HOMERUNS _____ GRANDSLAMS _____ RBI'S

_____ STOLEN BASES _____ OUTS _____ STRIKEOUTS

ON DEFENSE I HAD:

_____ CATCHES _____ DOUBLE PLAYS _____ ERRORS

_____ OUTS _____ GROUNDERS _____ POPFLIES

PITCHES:

_____ K'S _____ WALKS _____ HIT BATTER

_____ BALLS _____ STRIKES _____ TOTAL PITCHES

_____ WON _____ LOST _____ TIED _____ SCORE

GAME 5

DATE: _____

WE PLAYED AGAINST: _____

INNINGS I PLAYED: _____ POSITIONS I PLAYED: _____

FIELD I PLAYED ON: _____ POSITION I BATTED_____

ON OFFENSE I HAD:

_____ HITS _____ WALKS _____ HIT BY PITCHES

_____ SINGLES _____ DOUBLES _____ TRIPLES

_____ HOMERUNS _____ GRANDSLAMS _____ RBI'S

_____ STOLEN BASES _____ OUTS _____ STRIKEOUTS

ON DEFENSE I HAD:

_____ CATCHES _____ DOUBLE PLAYS _____ ERRORS

_____ OUTS _____ GROUNDERS _____ POPFLIES

PITCHES:

_____ K'S _____ WALKS _____ HIT BATTER

_____ BALLS _____ STRIKES _____ TOTAL PITCHES

_____WON _____LOST _____TIED _____ SCORE

GAME 6

DATE: _____

WE PLAYED AGAINST: _____

INNINGS I PLAYED: _____ POSITIONS I PLAYED: _____

FIELD I PLAYED ON: _____ POSITION I BATTED_____

ON OFFENSE I HAD:

_____ HITS _____ WALKS _____ HIT BY PITCHES

_____ SINGLES _____ DOUBLES _____ TRIPLES

_____ HOMERUNS _____ GRANDSLAMS _____ RBI'S

_____ STOLEN BASES _____ OUTS _____ STRIKEOUTS

ON DEFENSE I HAD:

_____ CATCHES _____ DOUBLE PLAYS _____ ERRORS

_____ OUTS _____GROUNDERS _____POPFLIES

PITCHES:

_____ K'S _____ WALKS _____ HIT BATTER

_____ BALLS _____ STRIKES _____ TOTAL PITCHES

_____WON _____LOST _____TIED _____ SCORE

PHOTOS:

GAME 7

DATE: _____

WE PLAYED AGAINST: _____

INNINGS I PLAYED: _____ POSITIONS I PLAYED: _____

FIELD I PLAYED ON: _____ POSITION I BATTED_____

ON OFFENSE I HAD:

_____ HITS _____ WALKS _____ HIT BY PITCHES

_____ SINGLES _____ DOUBLES _____ TRIPLES

_____ HOMERUNS _____ GRANDSLAMS _____ RBI'S

_____ STOLEN BASES _____ OUTS _____ STRIKEOUTS

ON DEFENSE I HAD:

_____ CATCHES _____ DOUBLE PLAYS _____ ERRORS

_____ OUTS _____GROUNDERS _____POPFLIES

PITCHES:

_____ K'S _____ WALKS _____ HIT BATTER

_____ BALLS _____ STRIKES _____ TOTAL PITCHES

_____WON _____LOST _____TIED _____ SCORE

GAME 8

DATE: _____

WE PLAYED AGAINST: _____

INNINGS I PLAYED: _____ POSITIONS I PLAYED: _____

FIELD I PLAYED ON: _____ POSITION I BATTED _____

ON OFFENSE I HAD:

_____ HITS _____ WALKS _____ HIT BY PITCHES

_____ SINGLES _____ DOUBLES _____ TRIPLES

_____ HOMERUNS _____ GRANDSLAMS _____ RBI'S

_____ STOLEN BASES _____ OUTS _____ STRIKEOUTS

ON DEFENSE I HAD:

_____ CATCHES _____ DOUBLE PLAYS _____ ERRORS

_____ OUTS _____ GROUNDERS _____ POPFLIES

PITCHES:

_____ K'S _____ WALKS _____ HIT BATTER

_____ BALLS _____ STRIKES _____ TOTAL PITCHES

_____ WON _____ LOST _____ TIED _____ SCORE

GAME 9

DATE: _____

WE PLAYED AGAINST: _____

INNINGS I PLAYED: _____ POSITIONS I PLAYED: _____

FIELD I PLAYED ON: _____ POSITION I BATTED_____

ON OFFENSE I HAD:

_____ HITS _____ WALKS _____ HIT BY PITCHES

_____ SINGLES _____ DOUBLES _____ TRIPLES

_____ HOMERUNS _____ GRANDSLAMS _____ RBI'S

_____ STOLEN BASES _____ OUTS _____ STRIKEOUTS

ON DEFENSE I HAD:

_____ CATCHES _____ DOUBLE PLAYS _____ ERRORS

_____ OUTS _____GROUNDERS _____POPFLIES

PITCHES:

_____ K'S _____ WALKS _____ HIT BATTER

_____ BALLS _____ STRIKES _____ TOTAL PITCHES

_____WON _____LOST _____TIED _____ SCORE

PHOTOS:

GAME 10

DATE: _____

WE PLAYED AGAINST: _____

INNINGS I PLAYED: _____ POSITIONS I PLAYED: _____

FIELD I PLAYED ON: _____ POSITION I BATTED_____

ON OFFENSE I HAD:

_____ HITS _____ WALKS _____ HIT BY PITCHES

_____ SINGLES _____ DOUBLES _____ TRIPLES

_____ HOMERUNS _____ GRANDSLAMS _____ RBI'S

_____ STOLEN BASES _____ OUTS _____ STRIKEOUTS

ON DEFENSE I HAD:

_____ CATCHES _____ DOUBLE PLAYS _____ ERRORS

_____ OUTS _____ GROUNDERS _____ POPFLIES

PITCHES:

_____ K'S _____ WALKS _____ HIT BATTER

_____ BALLS _____ STRIKES _____ TOTAL PITCHES

_____ WON _____ LOST _____ TIED _____ SCORE

GAME 11

DATE: _____

WE PLAYED AGAINST: _____

INNINGS I PLAYED: _____ POSITIONS I PLAYED: _____

FIELD I PLAYED ON: _____ POSITION I BATTED_____

ON OFFENSE I HAD:

_____ HITS _____ WALKS _____ HIT BY PITCHES

_____ SINGLES _____ DOUBLES _____ TRIPLES

_____ HOMERUNS _____ GRANDSLAMS _____ RBI'S

_____ STOLEN BASES _____ OUTS _____ STRIKEOUTS

ON DEFENSE I HAD:

_____ CATCHES _____ DOUBLE PLAYS _____ ERRORS

_____ OUTS _____ GROUNDERS _____ POPFLIES

PITCHES:

_____ K'S _____ WALKS _____ HIT BATTER

_____ BALLS _____ STRIKES _____ TOTAL PITCHES

_____WON _____LOST _____TIED _____ SCORE

GAME 12

DATE: _____

WE PLAYED AGAINST: _____

INNINGS I PLAYED: _____ POSITIONS I PLAYED: _____

FIELD I PLAYED ON: _____ POSITION I BATTED_____

ON OFFENSE I HAD:

_____ HITS _____ WALKS _____ HIT BY PITCHES

_____ SINGLES _____ DOUBLES _____ TRIPLES

_____ HOMERUNS _____ GRANDSLAMS _____ RBI'S

_____ STOLEN BASES _____ OUTS _____ STRIKEOUTS

ON DEFENSE I HAD:

_____ CATCHES _____ DOUBLE PLAYS _____ ERRORS

_____ OUTS _____ GROUNDERS _____ POPFLIES

PITCHES:

_____ K'S _____ WALKS _____ HIT BATTER

_____ BALLS _____ STRIKES _____ TOTAL PITCHES

_____ WON _____ LOST _____ TIED _____ SCORE

PHOTOS:

GAME 13

DATE: _____

WE PLAYED AGAINST: _____

INNINGS I PLAYED: _____ POSITIONS I PLAYED: _____

FIELD I PLAYED ON: _____ POSITION I BATTED_____

ON OFFENSE I HAD:

_____ HITS _____ WALKS _____ HIT BY PITCHES

_____ SINGLES _____ DOUBLES _____ TRIPLES

_____ HOMERUNS _____ GRANDSLAMS _____ RBI'S

_____ STOLEN BASES _____ OUTS _____ STRIKEOUTS

ON DEFENSE I HAD:

_____ CATCHES _____ DOUBLE PLAYS _____ ERRORS

_____ OUTS _____GROUNDERS _____POPFLIES

PITCHES:

_____ K'S _____ WALKS _____ HIT BATTER

_____ BALLS _____ STRIKES _____ TOTAL PITCHES

_____WON _____LOST _____TIED _____ SCORE

GAME 14

DATE: _____

WE PLAYED AGAINST: _____

INNINGS I PLAYED: _____ POSITIONS I PLAYED: _____

FIELD I PLAYED ON: _____ POSITION I BATTED_____

ON OFFENSE I HAD:

_____ HITS _____ WALKS _____ HIT BY PITCHES

_____ SINGLES _____ DOUBLES _____ TRIPLES

_____ HOMERUNS _____ GRANDSLAMS _____ RBI'S

_____ STOLEN BASES _____ OUTS _____ STRIKEOUTS

ON DEFENSE I HAD:

_____ CATCHES _____ DOUBLE PLAYS _____ ERRORS

_____ OUTS _____ GROUNDERS _____ POPFLIES

PITCHES:

_____ K'S _____ WALKS _____ HIT BATTER

_____ BALLS _____ STRIKES _____ TOTAL PITCHES

_____ WON _____ LOST _____ TIED _____ SCORE

GAME 15

DATE: _____

WE PLAYED AGAINST: _____

INNINGS I PLAYED: _____ POSITIONS I PLAYED: _____

FIELD I PLAYED ON: _____ POSITION I BATTED_____

ON OFFENSE I HAD:

_____ HITS _____ WALKS _____ HIT BY PITCHES

_____ SINGLES _____ DOUBLES _____ TRIPLES

_____ HOMERUNS _____ GRANDSLAMS _____ RBI'S

_____ STOLEN BASES _____ OUTS _____ STRIKEOUTS

ON DEFENSE I HAD:

_____ CATCHES _____ DOUBLE PLAYS _____ ERRORS

_____ OUTS _____GROUNDERS _____POPFLIES

PITCHES:

_____ K'S _____ WALKS _____ HIT BATTER

_____ BALLS _____ STRIKES _____ TOTAL PITCHES

_____WON _____LOST _____TIED _____ SCORE

PHOTOS:

GAME 16

DATE: _____

WE PLAYED AGAINST: _____

INNINGS I PLAYED: _____ POSITIONS I PLAYED: _____

FIELD I PLAYED ON: _____ POSITION I BATTED_____

ON OFFENSE I HAD:

_____ HITS _____ WALKS _____ HIT BY PITCHES

_____ SINGLES _____ DOUBLES _____ TRIPLES

_____ HOMERUNS _____ GRANDSLAMS _____ RBI'S

_____ STOLEN BASES _____ OUTS _____ STRIKEOUTS

ON DEFENSE I HAD:

_____ CATCHES _____ DOUBLE PLAYS _____ ERRORS

_____ OUTS _____GROUNDERS _____POPFLIES

PITCHES:

_____ K'S _____ WALKS _____ HIT BATTER

_____ BALLS _____ STRIKES _____ TOTAL PITCHES

_____WON _____LOST _____TIED _____ SCORE

GAME 17

DATE: _____

WE PLAYED AGAINST: _____

INNINGS I PLAYED: _____ POSITIONS I PLAYED: _____

FIELD I PLAYED ON: _____ POSITION I BATTED_____

ON OFFENSE I HAD:

_____ HITS _____ WALKS _____ HIT BY PITCHES

_____ SINGLES _____ DOUBLES _____ TRIPLES

_____ HOMERUNS _____ GRANDSLAMS _____ RBI'S

_____ STOLEN BASES _____ OUTS _____ STRIKEOUTS

ON DEFENSE I HAD:

_____ CATCHES _____ DOUBLE PLAYS _____ ERRORS

_____ OUTS _____GROUNDERS _____POPFLIES

PITCHES:

_____ K'S _____ WALKS _____ HIT BATTER

_____ BALLS _____ STRIKES _____ TOTAL PITCHES

_____WON _____LOST _____TIED _____ SCORE

GAME 18

DATE: _____

WE PLAYED AGAINST: _____

INNINGS I PLAYED: _____ POSITIONS I PLAYED: _____

FIELD I PLAYED ON: _____ POSITION I BATTED_____

ON OFFENSE I HAD:

_____ HITS _____ WALKS _____ HIT BY PITCHES

_____ SINGLES _____ DOUBLES _____ TRIPLES

_____ HOMERUNS _____ GRANDSLAMS _____ RBI'S

_____ STOLEN BASES _____ OUTS _____ STRIKEOUTS

ON DEFENSE I HAD:

_____ CATCHES _____ DOUBLE PLAYS _____ ERRORS

_____ OUTS _____GROUNDERS _____POPFLIES

PITCHES:

_____ K'S _____ WALKS _____ HIT BATTER

_____ BALLS _____ STRIKES _____ TOTAL PITCHES

_____WON _____LOST _____TIED _____ SCORE

PHOTOS:

GAME 19

DATE: _____

WE PLAYED AGAINST: _____

INNINGS I PLAYED: _____ POSITIONS I PLAYED: _____

FIELD I PLAYED ON: _____ POSITION I BATTED_____

ON OFFENSE I HAD:

_____ HITS _____ WALKS _____ HIT BY PITCHES

_____ SINGLES _____ DOUBLES _____ TRIPLES

_____ HOMERUNS _____ GRANDSLAMS _____ RBI'S

_____ STOLEN BASES _____ OUTS _____ STRIKEOUTS

ON DEFENSE I HAD:

_____ CATCHES _____ DOUBLE PLAYS _____ ERRORS

_____ OUTS _____ GROUNDERS _____ POPFLIES

PITCHES:

_____ K'S _____ WALKS _____ HIT BATTER

_____ BALLS _____ STRIKES _____ TOTAL PITCHES

_____ WON _____ LOST _____ TIED _____ SCORE

GAME 20

DATE: _____

WE PLAYED AGAINST: _____

INNINGS I PLAYED: _____ POSITIONS I PLAYED: _____

FIELD I PLAYED ON: _____ POSITION I BATTED_____

ON OFFENSE I HAD:

_____ HITS _____ WALKS _____ HIT BY PITCHES

_____ SINGLES _____ DOUBLES _____ TRIPLES

_____ HOMERUNS _____ GRANDSLAMS _____ RBI'S

_____ STOLEN BASES _____ OUTS _____ STRIKEOUTS

ON DEFENSE I HAD:

_____ CATCHES _____ DOUBLE PLAYS _____ ERRORS

_____ OUTS _____GROUNDERS _____POPFLIES

PITCHES:

_____ K'S _____ WALKS _____ HIT BATTER

_____ BALLS _____ STRIKES _____ TOTAL PITCHES

_____WON _____LOST _____TIED _____ SCORE

GAME 21

DATE: _____

WE PLAYED AGAINST: _____

INNINGS I PLAYED: _____ POSITIONS I PLAYED: _____

FIELD I PLAYED ON: _____ POSITION I BATTED_____

ON OFFENSE I HAD:

_____ HITS _____ WALKS _____ HIT BY PITCHES

_____ SINGLES _____ DOUBLES _____ TRIPLES

_____ HOMERUNS _____ GRANDSLAMS _____ RBI'S

_____ STOLEN BASES _____ OUTS _____ STRIKEOUTS

ON DEFENSE I HAD:

_____ CATCHES _____ DOUBLE PLAYS _____ ERRORS

_____ OUTS _____GROUNDERS _____POPFLIES

PITCHES:

_____ K'S _____ WALKS _____ HIT BATTER

_____ BALLS _____ STRIKES _____ TOTAL PITCHES

_____WON _____LOST _____TIED _____ SCORE

PHOTOS:

GAME 22

DATE: _____

WE PLAYED AGAINST: _____

INNINGS I PLAYED: _____ POSITIONS I PLAYED: _____

FIELD I PLAYED ON: _____ POSITION I BATTED_____

ON OFFENSE I HAD:

_____ HITS _____ WALKS _____ HIT BY PITCHES

_____ SINGLES _____ DOUBLES _____ TRIPLES

_____ HOMERUNS _____ GRANDSLAMS _____ RBI'S

_____ STOLEN BASES _____ OUTS _____ STRIKEOUTS

ON DEFENSE I HAD:

_____ CATCHES _____ DOUBLE PLAYS _____ ERRORS

_____ OUTS _____GROUNDERS _____POPFLIES

PITCHES:

_____ K'S _____ WALKS _____ HIT BATTER

_____ BALLS _____ STRIKES _____ TOTAL PITCHES

_____WON _____LOST _____TIED _____ SCORE

GAME 23

DATE: _____

WE PLAYED AGAINST: _____

INNINGS I PLAYED: _____ POSITIONS I PLAYED: _____

FIELD I PLAYED ON: _____ POSITION I BATTED_____

ON OFFENSE I HAD:

_____ HITS _____ WALKS _____ HIT BY PITCHES

_____ SINGLES _____ DOUBLES _____ TRIPLES

_____ HOMERUNS _____ GRANDSLAMS _____ RBI'S

_____ STOLEN BASES _____ OUTS _____ STRIKEOUTS

ON DEFENSE I HAD:

_____ CATCHES _____ DOUBLE PLAYS _____ ERRORS

_____ OUTS _____ GROUNDERS _____ POPFLIES

PITCHES:

_____ K'S _____ WALKS _____ HIT BATTER

_____ BALLS _____ STRIKES _____ TOTAL PITCHES

_____WON _____LOST _____TIED _____ SCORE

GAME 24

DATE: _____

WE PLAYED AGAINST: _____

INNINGS I PLAYED: _____ POSITIONS I PLAYED: _____

FIELD I PLAYED ON: _____ POSITION I BATTED_____

ON OFFENSE I HAD:

_____ HITS _____ WALKS _____ HIT BY PITCHES

_____ SINGLES _____ DOUBLES _____ TRIPLES

_____ HOMERUNS _____ GRANDSLAMS _____ RBI'S

_____ STOLEN BASES _____ OUTS _____ STRIKEOUTS

ON DEFENSE I HAD:

_____ CATCHES _____ DOUBLE PLAYS _____ ERRORS

_____ OUTS _____GROUNDERS _____POPFLIES

PITCHES:

_____ K'S _____ WALKS _____ HIT BATTER

_____ BALLS _____ STRIKES _____ TOTAL PITCHES

_____WON _____LOST _____TIED _____ SCORE

GAME 25

DATE: _____

WE PLAYED AGAINST: _____

INNINGS I PLAYED: _____ POSITIONS I PLAYED: _____

FIELD I PLAYED ON: _____ POSITION I BATTED _____

ON OFFENSE I HAD:

_____ HITS _____ WALKS _____ HIT BY PITCHES

_____ SINGLES _____ DOUBLES _____ TRIPLES

_____ HOMERUNS _____ GRANDSLAMS _____ RBI'S

_____ STOLEN BASES _____ OUTS _____ STRIKEOUTS

ON DEFENSE I HAD:

_____ CATCHES _____ DOUBLE PLAYS _____ ERRORS

_____ OUTS _____ GROUNDERS _____ POPFLIES

PITCHES:

_____ K'S _____ WALKS _____ HIT BATTER

_____ BALLS _____ STRIKES _____ TOTAL PITCHES

_____ WON _____ LOST _____ TIED _____ SCORE

MY END OF SEASON STATS

AVERAGES:

ON OFFENSE I HAD:

_____ HITS _____ WALKS _____ HIT BY PITCHES

_____ SINGLES _____ DOUBLES _____ TRIPLES

_____ HOMERUNS _____ GRANDSLAMS _____ RBI'S

_____ STOLEN BASES _____ OUTS _____ STRIKEOUTS

ON DEFENSE I HAD:

_____ CATCHES _____ DOUBLE PLAYS _____ ERRORS

_____ OUTS _____ GROUNDERS _____ POPFLIES

PITCHES:

_____ K'S _____ WALKS _____ HIT BATTER

_____ BALLS _____ STRIKES _____ TOTAL PITCHES

_____ WINS _____ LOSSES _____ TIES

_____ AVERAGE SCORE

MY TEAMMATES AUTOGRAPHS

FASTBALLS

HOMERUNS

LINE DRIVES

BUNTS

DEFENSE

STEALS

DETERMINATION

MY TEAMMATES AUTOGRAPHS

CATCHER

OFFENSE

SHORTSTOP

OUTFIELD

INFIELD

PITCHER

GIRL POWER

THE M·V·P· ON MY TEAM IS:

_____

THE BEST PLAY I MADE THIS YEAR IS:

_____

MY FAVORITE GAME WAS AGAINST:

_____

I PRACTICE _____ TIMES PER WEEK

WHAT I LEARNED THIS SEASON:

_____

_____

_____

MY FAVORITE MEMORIES FROM THIS SEASON:

_____

_____

_____

MY COACHES COMMENTS:

_____

_____

_____

_____

MY PHOTOS

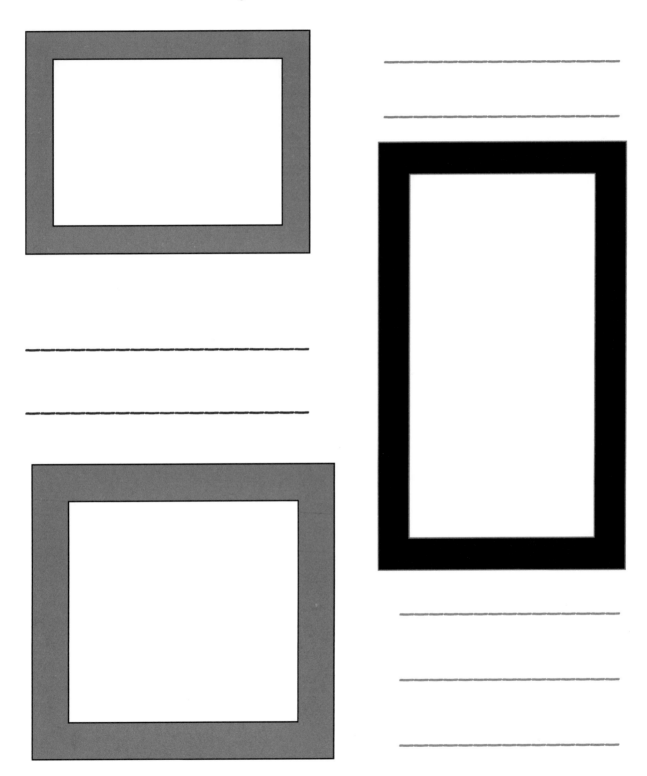

ME AND MY FRIENDS

PHOTOS:

PHOTOS:

COMMENTS:

COMMENTS:

PARENTS PAGE

31892264R00028

Made in the USA
San Bernardino, CA
22 March 2016

MW00929645

LEADER GUIDE

exhale

LOSE WHO YOU'RE NOT

LOVE WHO YOU ARE

LIVE YOUR ONE LIFE WELL

AMY CARROLL,

CHERI GREGORY

& TEAM

Exhale Leader Guide
ISBN-13: 9781099276934

Copyright ©2019 Amy Carroll & Cheri Gregory
All rights reserved

All Scripture quotations are marked with the version that they are taken from and pulled from https://www.biblegateway.com/.

Published with permission from Bethany House Publishing.

Dearest Leader,

We've been in your shoes, carefully choosing a study for a group of women we love. Knowing that it's our sacred responsibility to shepherd a small tribe for a season of their lives. Trusting God to do the big work after we've done faith-filled groundwork.

Because we've both led small groups, we have the utmost respect and love for you, not just in an abstract way but in a very substantial way. *Exhale* was birthed with a desire to see it used in small groups, and before the first word was written, we've been praying for you.

All we leader-types know that the women around us are tired. We hear the exhaustion in their conversations, and we see it on their precious faces.

We also feel their discouragement, women trying to be all things for all people all the time because it seems like the right thing to do. The *Christian* thing to do. But if this is the correct path, why the nagging sense that there should be more to life?

So many women spend their days trying to do too much for too many. Tragically, the long to-do lists they're tackling don't even include the tasks for which they were created! Thus, the exhaustion, that never-ending feeling of running-on-empty.

In contrast, the God-ordained good works for which we're made are life-giving, not draining. While they'll leave us tired, it's that satisfying sense of being spent-and-content.

Discerning the difference requires living examined lives.

We've found a process that helps each woman live her one life well. It doesn't entail a lot of how-tos. Instead, it contains transformational heart-tos, a new way of reflecting and acting that leads to better living.

We wrote this group study and guide, because this process of change is more powerful in a group where women can support, pray for, and challenge each other. Thank you for leading such a group!

Our prayer is that this leader guide and the videos we've made make your job simpler and more pleasurable. We know what a commitment you've made in leading, and we're praying for God's strength and delight to wash over you.

In His Love,

Amy & Cheri

Notes:

Study Schedule

GROUP GATHERINGS

IN THIS LEADER GUIDE:

You have the same material your participants have in their Study Guide. In addition, for each Group Gathering there's a Leader's Section with icebreakers and Extra Resources. We know how busy leaders are, so we want to make it as easy as possible for you.

ON THE NEXT PAGE:

You'll find a suggested schedule for an hour-long group gathering. You can expand these times if you meet longer.

Note: Group Gathering #1 will be a little different since there are no reading questions to discuss yet, so we've included a unique schedule for that week.

IF THE GROUP IS LARGE:

You may want to break into smaller discussion groups of less than 10. In this case, you can provide starter questions for the group and then let them choose their favorites from the Study Guide for that week. It's also a great idea to assign a small group leader who will keep the conversation flowing.

GROUP STUDY GUIDE:

Each member of the group needs a copy of *Exhale* and the Exhale Group Study Guide. Links to both can be found at ExhaleBook.com/Study.

WE'D LOVE TO HEAR FROM YOU ALONG THE WAY!

Stories of how God uses the book are what keep us fueled up for more ministry. Please visit us at ExhaleBook.com/Study and leave your story or comments about how the group study impacted your participants. We look forward to hearing how it went!

© AMY CARROLL & CHERI GREGORY

Group Gathering Schedule

10 Minutes-- Icebreaker Time:

For this study, group bonding and trust are important. Members will be sharing their lives and struggles, so they need to feel connected and safe. We've designed these with increasing depth (plus a dose of fun!) over the six gatherings. If you'd like to have other questions as an option, the book *The Complete Book of Questions* by Garry D. Poole is a fabulous resource you can use for this and many other occasions.

15-20 Minutes-- Video Teaching:

We have a set of free teaching videos, and you can access all of them at ExhaleBook.com/Study. Each of these videos uses Scripture to expound on a concept taught in the week's chapters.

20-25 Minutes-- Discussion:

Because you know your group best, here's where your leadership really counts! Choose questions from the week's work where you'd like to focus discussion time. You can also involve your participants by asking them to mark the questions that most connect with their heart to discuss during the next group gathering.

10 Minutes-- Small group prayer:

Either within the smaller discussion groups or in groups of 3-4, ask members to share personal prayer concerns. Our suggestion is to direct members to keep requests personal or within their immediate family to avoid deflecting attention to "Aunt Suzie's best friend's dog." "Share short and pray long" is another encouragement that helps to keep prayer the main activity during this time. Some weeks, just to give you options, we'll give a suggestion for a fresh way to conduct prayer time at the end.

© Amy Carroll & Cheri Gregory

Notes:

© Amy Carroll & Cheri Gregory

GROUP GATHERING #1

Meet & Greet

SUGGESTED SUPPLIES:

Nametags, pens or markers, coffee bar (optional), snacks (optional), candy for icebreaker (see link)

5-10 MINUTES-- ARRIVAL:

Have a coffee bar and/or snacks for this first gathering so women can mingle and chat as they arrive. It will leave you freed up to great everyone, point out a nametag station, and distribute books as needed

10 MINUTES-- ICEBREAKER:

Play the Great Candy Pass Game. (There are lots of other icebreakers at this website. Feel free to choose another if you'd like!) https://womensministrytoolbox.com/icebreaker-the-great-candy-pass/

15 MINUTES-- INTRODUCTIONS:

Ask each woman in the circle to tell her name and one thing she'd like the group to know about her. Do one more pass and ask each woman to share what she hopes to gain from participation in this small group.

10 MINUTES-- LEADER SHARE:

Tell why you chose *Exhale* for this small group and any of the features that you've seen so far that make you excited about this book and study.

20 MINUTES-- VIDEO:

Show introductory video. Link found at ExhaleBook.com/Study.

5 MINUTES–

Go through the assignment for the week.

THIS WEEK

The group will read the Introduction through Chapter 3. Explain that there are questions in the Study Guide for each chapter, but the essential parts for each week are the daily "Now Breathe" exercises and the "Square Breathing Time" exercise at the end of the week. Encourage the women to come each week, even if their schedule kept them from answering all the questions, so that they grow together.

© AMY CARROLL & CHERI GREGORY

Notes:

© Amy Carroll & Cheri Gregory

WEEK 1

Lose Who You're Not

Before we can step into a better life, we have to declutter the one we have, eliminating all the things that we were never called to do or be in the first place. We want to recognize all the things we've become that aren't our truest, God-created self.

We encourage you to highlight or underline anything that hits the center of your heart. At the end of the week, there will be a whole day scheduled to process what you've learned and what God has spoken to you.

We want you to process this book slowly so that the truths in it have time to take root and make a difference. Check off the tasks as you go but don't rush. We don't want *Exhale* just to be the title of the book. We want it to be the way you experience the book.

In that spirit, use this Participant's Guide in a way that leads you to exhale. We know that some of you will want to answer every question, but some of you may be in a phase of life that All The Questions make you hyperventilate. If that's you, then just complete the "Just Breathe" activity at the end of each chapter as well as the "Square Breathing Time" and "The Breathing Space" in each section. These are the key exercises that will lead to the change you long for.

Let's get started! Change is hard, but it's possible.

Day 1:

_____ READ THE INTRODUCTION

_____ ANSWER THE QUESTIONS

When you're lying awake worrying, fretting, and/or planning in the middle of the night, what are you thinking about?

© AMY CARROLL & CHERI GREGORY

We say, "You are created for less. Less worry, less over-attempting, less problem-preventing, less second-guessing." What do you want less of?

We also say, "You are created for more. More joy, more pure happiness, more fulfillment, more deep relationship." Which of these made your heart flutter with hope, knowing that you need more of this?

What else would you like more of?

In the deepest part of your heart, what do you hope to gain from reading, reflecting on, and discussing this book?

© AMY CARROLL & CHERI GREGORY

Day 2:

_____READ CHAPTER 1

_____COMPLETE "NOW BREATHE" AT THE END OF THE CHAPTER *(THERE IS A SINGLE "NOW BREATHE" QUESTION AT THE END OF EACH CHAPTER IN THE BOOK.)*

_____ANSWER THE QUESTIONS

My "Now Breathe" Notes:

© AMY CARROLL & CHERI GREGORY

How do you feel when you read that change in your heart, mind, soul and spirit is possible?

a. Excited — because although you feel stuck right now, you're looking forward to a new way of living?

b. Resistant — like you want to dig in your heels because *I'm fine just the way I am thank you very much*?

c. Overwhelmed or paralyzed — you know something isn't working in your life, but you have no idea what to change or even how to make changes happen?

d. Afraid — because you're worried that you might try but fail?

Review the story of Zacchaeus in Luke 19:1-10. Zacchaeus wanted to know Jesus, and he wanted to experience Jesus for himself. Why do you think this was foundational in Zacchaeus' change?

Is this the same as or different from the way you've approached change? How?

How does it look different when we see ourselves as the change agent versus resting in the truth that God is the only way that change is possible? Note: The word "change" carries a different type of weight when we are striving to please God than when we know we already please Him.

© AMY CARROLL & CHERI GREGORY

At the end of the chapter, how did the summary "You're NOT permanently stuck" hit you? Do you believe it? Why or why not?

A BREATH OF FRESH AIR

If you'd like to hear more related to this topic, you can listen to Episode #136 of

Grit 'n' Grace "When You Need to Leave Your Comfort Zone" at

https://gritngracegirls.com/episode136

© AMY CARROLL & CHERI GREGORY

Day 3:

_____READ CHAPTER 2

_____COMPLETE "NOW BREATHE" AT THE END OF THE CHAPTER

_____ANSWER THE QUESTIONS

My "Now Breathe" Notes:

© AMY CARROLL & CHERI GREGORY

Think about a time you failed. What emotions surround that experience?

How has the lie that "nothing's worse than making mistakes; nothing's worse than failure" fueled your fears?

Review the story of Peter walking on the water in Matthew 14:25-33. How does the concept of competent mistakes and the story of Peter walking on the water change the way you think about failure?

© AMY CARROLL & CHERI GREGORY

How will your life change as you trust God with your mistakes?

At the end of the chapter, how did the summary "You're NOT required to be perfect" hit you? Do you believe it? Why or why not?

A BREATH OF FRESH AIR

If you'd like to hear more related to this topic, you can listen to Episode #111 of

Grit 'n' Grace "Finding Peace that Calms Your Fear-Filled Heart" at

https://gritngracegirls.com/episode111

© AMY CARROLL & CHERI GREGORY

Day 4:

_____Read chapter 3

_____Complete "Now Breathe" at the end of the chapter

_____Answer the questions

My "Now Breathe" Notes:

© Amy Carroll & Cheri Gregory

What are some "plates of trash" that have been handed to you in the past?

What inappropriate expectations of yourself have you held in the past?

List some lies that are influencing your decisions now. For example: *I am responsible for my family's happiness, so I have to say yes to their requests.*

Review Jesus' interactions with John the Baptist's disciples in Luke 7:18-35. From today's lessons from Jesus, what truths can you have ready to smother those lies?

© AMY CARROLL & CHERI GREGORY

At the end of the chapter, how did the summary "You're NOT responsible for everyone all the time" hit you? Do you believe it? Why or why not?

A BREATH OF FRESH AIR

If you'd like to hear more related to this topic, you can listen to Episode #127 of

Grit 'n' Grace "From Dismal Failure to Grit 'n' Grace" at

https://gritngracegirls.com/episode127

© AMY CARROLL & CHERI GREGORY

_____SQUARE BREATHING TIME

At the beginning of Section 2, Love Who You Are, Amy describes a breathing exercise called Square Breathing. If you want to flip there now and read it, feel free. Square breathing is a repetitive exercise that slows your heart, evens your breath, and relaxes your body. This last day in the week's study is simply to repeat what you've already learned so that you can relax into it.

Let today strengthen your heart, slow your breath, and build confidence that God is working in you!

Go back through the chapters you read this week. If you missed any parts, feel free to complete them now.

Write out your favorite quotes and concepts from the Introduction through Chapter 3.

© AMY CARROLL & CHERI GREGORY

Put a star by the summary sentence where you've made the most progress this week. Circle the one that you still need to grasp in a deeper way.

You're not permanently stuck.

You're not required to be perfect.

You're not responsible for everyone all the time.

Write out a prayer below. Ask God to do His work in you until it's completed. Ask Him for clarity and strength for the difficult truths.

exhale.

© Amy Carroll & Cheri Gregory

Notes:

© Amy Carroll & Cheri Gregory

GROUP GATHERING #2

Supplies Needed:

High school photos, 1 notecard for each person (for prayer time)

10 Minutes -- Icebreaker:

Have each woman share her high school picture and tell about how her style has changed from then to now. If a woman didn't bring a picture, just let her describe her high school look. (Leaders, you start and let them laugh with you first. Make sure nobody feels belittled, but this can sure bring lots of laughter!)

15-20 Minutes – Video Teaching #2:

Access it at ExhaleBook.com/Study

20-25 Minutes --

Discussion

10 Minutes – Small Group Prayer:

Ask each woman to add her name to the top of her notecard and to write a personal prayer request that she's willing to share with another person on her card. Ask each person to pass her card to the right. In the silence, ask the women to pray for the request on the card she just received. If you have time, pass the cards to the right every few minutes and give time to pray. The card that you end with is to take home and pray for over the course of the week.

© Amy Carroll & Cheri Gregory

Notes:

© Amy Carroll & Cheri Gregory

Lose Who You're Not

Day 1:

_____Read chapter 4

_____Complete "Now Breathe" at the end of the chapter

_____Answer the questions

My "Now Breathe" Notes:

© Amy Carroll & Cheri Gregory

Cheri talked about a defining moment that she labeled "rejection." Think of a defining moment in your life. How would you label it: control, not good enough, fear, shame, perfectionism?

How does that defining moment affect the way you make everyday decisions?

How does it affect your relationships?

Read Ephesians 1: 1-14 and underline all words that describe how Jesus sees you. How does it feel to replace the lies and fears with God's truths about you in Ephesians 1?

© AMY CARROLL & CHERI GREGORY

At the end of the chapter, how did the summary "You're NOT defined by old labels" hit you? Do you believe it? Why or why not?

A BREATH OF FRESH AIR

If you'd like to hear more related to this topic, you can listen to Episode #10 of

Grit 'n' Grace "Overcoming Error Terror" at

https://gritngracegirls.com/episode10

© AMY CARROLL & CHERI GREGORY

Day 2:

_____Read chapter 5

_____Complete "Now Breathe" at the end of the chapter

_____Answer the questions

My "Now Breathe" Notes:

© Amy Carroll & Cheri Gregory

Record your thoughts on the Principle of Intention. How does it make you feel when you read the guidelines: "Do what God says to do and say what He says to say"?

- relieved?
- restricted?
- fearful?
- frustrated?
- content?
- purposeful?

Review the story of Jesus in the temple in Luke 2:41-52. Describe a time in your life when you successfully set a boundary by being about your Father's business. How did it feel? How did the other person respond?

Amy described needing a written contract to form and keep her boundaries. What do you typically need to "stick to something"?

Who is someone you can trust with helping you to stick to a boundary? Who can walk along beside you and encourage you and remind you of truth?

© AMY CARROLL & CHERI GREGORY

At the end of the chapter, how did the summary "You're NOT boundaryless" hit you? Do you believe it? Why or why not?

A BREATH OF FRESH AIR

If you'd like to read more about this topic, visit Amy's blog and read "Why You SHOULD Think of Yourself When You Give." You can find it at https://amycarroll.org/why-you-should-think-of-yourself-when-you-give/

© AMY CARROLL & CHERI GREGORY

Day 3:

_____READ CHAPTER 6

_____COMPLETE "NOW BREATHE" AT THE END OF THE CHAPTER

_____ANSWER THE QUESTIONS

My "Now Breathe" Notes:

© AMY CARROLL & CHERI GREGORY

Review the story of Rebekah in Genesis 25-27. Think of an example when you offered unasked for advice. Be honest with yourself as you think about what your true motive was. How did you give the advice? Did you passively sneak it in? Did you yell it out? Did you ask permission?

How did the other person respond?

Name a problem that you're dying to fix.

Use the table in chapter 6 that contrasts helping with meddling. With these definitions, will it be helping or meddling to get involved in this problem? If it's helping, write a prayer here to intervene in a godly, loving way. If it's meddling, write a prayer here asking God for strength to stay out of it. (We know… painful!)

© AMY CARROLL & CHERI GREGORY

At the end of the chapter, how did the summary "You're NOT the fixer of every problem" hit you? Do you believe it? Why or why not?

A BREATH OF FRESH AIR

If you'd like to hear more related to this topic, Cheri has written a helpful blog post on this topic called "How to Know if You are Helping, Meddling, or Rescuing" at

https://cherigregory.com/being-helpful/

© AMY CARROLL & CHERI GREGORY

Day 4:

_____ READ CHAPTER 7

_____ COMPLETE "NOW BREATHE" AT THE END OF THE CHAPTER

_____ ANSWER THE QUESTIONS

My "Now Breathe" Notes:

© AMY CARROLL & CHERI GREGORY

Review the story of Peter's denials and Jesus' look in Luke 22: 24-62. Describe how you think God looks at you—the expression on His face—when you do something good. How about when you do something wrong?

What beliefs about God drive these beliefs about how He responds to you?

Deep down, do you believe that God is asking you to change or that He is changing you? How does believing the truth, that we can only participate with God's changing power, shift your perspective on your ability to break cyclical sin?

Remember and describe a time when you've experienced the gift of repentance and the power of grace in your life.

© AMY CARROLL & CHERI GREGORY

At the end of the chapter, how did the summary "You're NOT a hopeless case" hit you? Do you believe it? Why or why not?

A BREATH OF FRESH AIR

If you'd like to hear more related to this topic, you can listen to Episode #102 of Grit 'n' Grace "How to Level Up Through the Power of Simple Truths" at

https://gritngracegirls.com/episode102

– 38 –

© AMY CARROLL & CHERI GREGORY

Day 5:

_____SQUARE BREATHING TIME

This last day in the week's study is simply to repeat what you've already learned so that you can relax into it.

Let today strengthen your heart, slow your breath, and build confidence that God is working in you!

Go back through the chapters you read this week. If you missed any parts, feel free to complete them now.

Write out your favorite quotes and concepts from the Introduction through Chapter 4-7.

© AMY CARROLL & CHERI GREGORY

Put a star by the summary sentence where you've made the most progress this week. Circle the one that you still need to grasp in a deeper way.

> You're not defined by old labels.
>
> You're not boundaryless.
>
> You're not the fixer of every problem.
>
> You're not a hopeless case.

Write out a prayer below. Ask God to do His work in you until it's completed. Ask Him for clarity and strength for the difficult truths.

exhale

© AMY CARROLL & CHERI GREGORY

Notes:

© Amy Carroll & Cheri Gregory

GROUP GATHERING #3

SUPPLIES NEEDED:

2 balls for the icebreaker activity (round fruit works too)

10 MINUTES-- ICEBREAKER:

Have two lines of women race to pass a ball person to person under their chin to the end of the line. (Yep! We know it's a game from childhood. Encourage your group to cut loose and have fun.) Discuss what it feels like to break personal space and boundaries in the game. How about in real life?

15-20 MINUTES– VIDEO TEACHING #3:

Access it at ExhaleBook.com/Study

20-25 MINUTES--

Discussion

10 MINUTES– SMALL GROUP PRAYER:

Let small groups "share short and pray long" with personal prayer requests.

© AMY CARROLL & CHERI GREGORY

Notes:

© Amy Carroll & Cheri Gregory

We have heard many protests over this section of the book.

- o "Loving who I am seems so self-centered."
- o "I'd have to think far too much about myself to figure out my gifts."
- o "I can't love who I am. I'm sinful after all!"

We've heard each objection, and we understand the root of the problem.

Coming to the place where we all agree requires clarity, so let's start by defining what we mean by "love who you are." We mean that each of us is to love the person that God created us to be, the being (you!) who makes Him break into a Divine ear-to-ear grin with just one thought of you. The you who He's imbued with gifts and interwoven with good works to do.

God loves you deeply, unconditionally, and irrevocably, so it's not only okay to love who you are, it's essential. It's actually a gift of worship for your Creator.

As uncomfortable as it might be, this is the time to focus on you, not for your own glory, but to find out how you can better glorify God. Go slow. Ask Him to show you what you need to learn. Try to see yourself through God's eyes. Love who you are.

Day 1:

_____READ CHAPTER 8

_____COMPLETE "NOW BREATHE" AT THE END OF THE CHAPTER

_____ANSWER THE QUESTIONS

© AMY CARROLL & CHERI GREGORY

My "Now Breathe" Notes:

Make a list of the authorities in your life: both good and bad.

© AMY CARROLL & CHERI GREGORY

After reviewing the story of the man born blind in John 9:1-38, underline people who you have given authority to that you need to dis-appoint. Circle the authorities who are given by God and positive.

What is one step you can take this week to dis-appoint someone that is underlined? Remember, this may only be a decision you make, not necessarily an action toward someone else.

What is keeping you from making that change or taking charge?

© AMY CARROLL & CHERI GREGORY

At the end of the chapter, how did the summary "You ARE a limited edition of one" hit you? Do you believe that's true? Why or why not?

A BREATH OF FRESH AIR

If you'd like to hear more related to this topic, you can listen to Episode #88 of

Grit 'n' Grace "Walking Out Your Unique, Powerful Story" at

https://gritngracegirls.com/episode88

© AMY CARROLL & CHERI GREGORY

Day 2:

_____ READ CHAPTER 9

_____ COMPLETE "NOW BREATHE" AT THE END OF THE CHAPTER

_____ ANSWER THE QUESTIONS

My "Now Breathe" Notes:

© AMY CARROLL & CHERI GREGORY

What parts of your personal story (your life events) have made you feel like you're "not enough," or that you're "too much?"

Review the story of the Canaanite woman in Matthew 15:21-28. Use one of the negative items in the list you just made to fill in the blank:

I wish I were _____.

Now switch it to a statement of gratitude that will build your fortitude.

I'm thankful I'm _____.

What are some things about your life's story that could be helpful to another struggling woman?

© AMY CARROLL & CHERI GREGORY

How can you begin to own that story and use it to empower another person this week?

At the end of the chapter, how did the summary "You ARE a woman with a story linked to His" hit you? Do you believe that's true? Why or why not?

A BREATH OF FRESH AIR

If you'd like to hear more related to this topic, you can listen to Episode #123 of Grit 'n' Grace "Get Up and Go - The World Needs Your Story" at https://gritngracegirls.com/episode123

© AMY CARROLL & CHERI GREGORY

Day 3:

_____Read chapter 10

_____Complete "Now Breathe" at the end of the chapter

_____Answer the questions

My "Now Breathe" Notes:

© Amy Carroll & Cheri Gregory

After taking the quiz at the back of the book or at ExhaleBook.com, which personality type did you find that you are?

Were any of these traits present while you were growing up? Did you take on more of them at a certain transitional point in your life?

Review the story of Jesus' feeding of the five thousand in John 6:5-13. Describe a time when you faced a situation you found impossible, but, after praying and asking for help, you discovered a way through?

How would it change things to acknowledge the strengths that God has given you?

© AMY CARROLL & CHERI GREGORY

At the end of the chapter, how did the summary "You ARE gifted with God-given strengths" hit you? Do you believe it's true? Why or why not?

A BREATH OF FRESH AIR

If you'd like to hear more related to this topic, you can listen to Episode #137 of

Grit 'n' Grace "Leveraging God's Positive Power in You" at

https://gritngracegirls.com/episode137

© AMY CARROLL & CHERI GREGORY

Day 4:

_____ READ CHAPTER 11

_____ COMPLETE "NOW BREATHE" AT THE END OF THE CHAPTER

_____ ANSWER THE QUESTIONS

My "Now Breathe" Notes:

© AMY CARROLL & CHERI GREGORY

Review the story of Matthew's calling in Matthew 9:9-12. How has God used your "quirks" to qualify you in ways you never expected?

How have you been pursuing a "normal" lifestyle when God might be calling you to use your weirdness in wonderful ways to bring people to Jesus?

Reflect on your life experiences and skills. As you read your local paper, watch your local news, or think about the needs in your community, see if anything comes to your mind as a way you can connect with those in your community utilizing your unique quirks.

© AMY CARROLL & CHERI GREGORY

List 10 qualities that you possess that could have a positive impact on others. (These can be based on your personality, life experiences, training, hardships, quirks, etc.)

At the end of the chapter, how did the summary "You ARE beautifully quirky" hit you? Do you believe that it's true? Why or why not?

A BREATH OF FRESH AIR

If you'd like to hear more related to this topic, you can listen to Episodes #59 of

Grit 'n' Grace "Created to Be Different - Living an Extraordinary Life" at

https://gritngracegirls.com/episode59/

© AMY CARROLL & CHERI GREGORY

_____SQUARE BREATHING TIME

This last day of your week's preparation is simply to repeat what you've already learned so that you can relax into it.

Let today strengthen your heart, slow your breath, and build confidence that God is working in you!

Go back through the chapters you read this week. If you missed any parts, feel free to complete them now.

Write out your favorite quotes and concepts from Chapters 8-11

© AMY CARROLL & CHERI GREGORY

Put a star by the summary sentence where you've made the most progress this week. Circle the one that you still need to grasp in a deeper way.

You are a limited edition of one.

You are a woman with a story linked to His.

You are gifted with God-given strengths.

You are beautifully quirky.

Write out a prayer below. Ask God to do His work in you until it's completed. Ask Him for clarity and strength for the difficult truths.

exhale

© AMY CARROLL & CHERI GREGORY

Notes:

© Amy Carroll & Cheri Gregory

GROUP GATHERING #4

SUPPLIES NEEDED:

One slip of paper for each participant, bowl (or hat or small bag) for icebreaker, a copy of "Breathe a Prayer" for each person in the group found at ExhaleBook.com/Study

10 MINUTES-- ICEBREAKER:

On a slip of paper, have each member write down one thing that she would consider uniquely "weird" about herself. It may be what she likes to do, or eat, or how she spends time… maybe something she finds funny that others don't get sometimes. Have group throw these anonymous statements into a bowl and guess whose it is as each one is drawn and read.

15-20 MINUTES– VIDEO TEACHING #4:

Access it at ExhaleBook.com/Study

20-25 MINUTES--

Discussion

10 MINUTES– SMALL GROUP PRAYER:

Leader, quickly explain the idea of a breath prayer from the "Breathe a Prayer" handout (found at ExhaleBook.com/Study) and read some examples. Have each group member write a short breath prayer. Go around the group and read these prayers out loud. Silence in between for reflection is terrific.

© AMY CARROLL & CHERI GREGORY

Notes:

© Amy Carroll & Cheri Gregory

Love Who You Are

Day 1:

_____Read chapter 12

_____Complete "Now Breathe" at the end of the chapter

_____Answer the questions

My "Now Breathe" Notes:

© Amy Carroll & Cheri Gregory

Reread John 10:3-16. Meditate on the progression of ten actions that Cheri highlights. Record which of these actions impacted you most today and why.

From the list of spiritual gifts in this chapter, write down the gifts that God has given you.

How can you use these gifts to strengthen the body of Christ, the church, and the people around you?

© AMY CARROLL & CHERI GREGORY

Who in your life needs to see you *be yourself* so that they have permission to be more of themselves? Write one practical way that you can give them that gift this week.

At the end of the chapter, how did the summary "You ARE essential to the body of Christ" hit you? Do you believe that you are? Why or why not?

A BREATH OF FRESH AIR

If you'd like to hear more related to this topic, you can read Cheri's blog post "How to Be the Best at Just Being Me" at https://cherigregory.com/just-being-me/

© AMY CARROLL & CHERI GREGORY

Day 2:

_____Read chapter 13

_____Complete "Now Breathe" at the end of the chapter

_____Answer the questions

My "Now Breathe" Notes:

© Amy Carroll & Cheri Gregory

Review the two stories of Jesus asking "What do you want me to do for you?" in Mark 10: 35-36, 46-51. If Jesus was standing in front of you today asking that question, how would you answer Him?

What has caused you to doubt that God has planted the desires of your heart and can bring them to reality?

Write a truth from today's Scripture (or any other that comes to mind) that exposes that doubt as a lie.

List the callings of your life from each season. At the end of the list, add a dream for the future.

© AMY CARROLL & CHERI GREGORY

At the end of the chapter, how did the summary "You ARE a woman with a current calling" hit you? Do you believe that you are? Why or why not?

A BREATH OF FRESH AIR

If you'd like to hear more related to this topic, you can listen to Episodes #82 of

Grit 'n' Grace "How to Handle Conflict with Confidence" at

https://gritngracegirls.com/episode82

© AMY CARROLL & CHERI GREGORY

Day 3:

_____READ CHAPTER 14

_____COMPLETE "NOW BREATHE" AT THE END OF THE CHAPTER

_____ANSWER THE QUESTIONS

My "Now Breathe" Notes:

© AMY CARROLL & CHERI GREGORY

Tell about a time you tried to impress other people.

Tell about a time that you judged someone else as an unimpressive person.

Review the parable of the lost sheep in Luke 15:4-7. How does it feel to shift yourself from being one of the 99 to being in The One Club?

Is there anyone in your life who you can completely let go in front of and be yourself? How can you be that person for someone else, reassuring them that they can be themselves *and* be loved?

© AMY CARROLL & CHERI GREGORY

At the end of the chapter, how did the summary "You ARE the one Jesus seeks" hit you? Do you believe you are? Why or why not?

A BREATH OF FRESH AIR

If you'd like to hear more related to this topic, you can listen to Episodes #101 of

Grit 'n' Grace "Seeking the Simple to Find the Rich and Deep" at

https://gritngracegirls.com/episode101/

© AMY CARROLL & CHERI GREGORY

Day 4:

_____SQUARE BREATHING TIME

Repeat what you've already learned so that you can relax into it. Let today strengthen your heart, slow your breath, and build confidence that God is working in you!

Go back through the chapters you read this week. If you missed any parts, feel free to complete them now.

Write out your favorite quotes and concepts from Chapters 12-14.

What ideas and/or truths are you still struggling through?

© AMY CARROLL & CHERI GREGORY

Put a star by the summary sentence where you've made the most progress this week. Circle the one that you still need to grasp in a deeper way.

You are essential to the body of Christ.

You are a woman with a current calling.

You are the one Jesus seeks.

Write out a prayer below. Ask God to do His work in you until it's completed. Ask Him for clarity and strength for the difficult truths.

© AMY CARROLL & CHERI GREGORY

Day 5:

_____THE BREATHING SPACE

Meditate on this verse, Psalm 18:19, "He [God] brought me out into a spacious place; he rescued me because he delighted in me." (NIV)

We want you to feel the spaciousness in this book and its process. It's definitely not our intent to smother you with One More Thing! Our last day this week will be set aside to simply reflect and process. Please use this time to allow the change that God is doing to soak deep into your soul.

From reading the chapters in section 1 and section 2, list the ways that you feel more equipped to lose who you're not and love who you are.

From reading and processing all the chapters so far, how will you better:

Glorify God?

Fulfill the longings of your heart?

Meet the needs of your people?

exhale

© AMY CARROLL & CHERI GREGORY

Notes:

© Amy Carroll & Cheri Gregory

GROUP GATHERING #5

SUPPLIES NEEDED:

None

10 MINUTES-- ICEBREAKER:

Have each member name 3 things she can't help but do (ie. sing, bake, craft, party plan, teach…)

15-20 MINUTES– VIDEO TEACHING #5:

Access it at ExhaleBook.com/Study

20-25 MINUTES--

Discussion

10 MINUTES– SMALL GROUP PRAYER:

Let small groups "share short and pray long" with personal prayer requests.

© AMY CARROLL & CHERI GREGORY

Notes:

© Amy Carroll & Cheri Gregory

You're almost to the end of the book, but the most important part is yet to come. All the decluttering you did to lose who you're not… And all the discovery you did to love who you are… those were important steps, but they aren't the destination.

Losing who you're not and loving who you are the steps that we put together for a purpose. They designed step one and step two so that you could make the most important leap of all: living your one life well.

Don't quit now! Remember the life we promised you at the beginning? A spent-and-content life to replace your running-on-empty life? You're ready for it now, but you have to step into it. Persevere and you'll see great rewards.

Day 1:

_____Read chapter 15

_____Complete "Now Breathe" at the end of the chapter

_____Answer the questions

My "Now Breathe" Notes:

© Amy Carroll & Cheri Gregory

Amy told about Mrs. Warren, an influential seed sender in her life, and she dedicated the book to her parents, her first and most important seed senders. Think about the seasons of your life. Who were the important seed senders in each? What makes these people memorable and important?

When you were a child?

As a new Christian?

Currently?

Review the seed parables in Mark 4. How do you feel knowing that you're called to sow alongside Jesus?

© AMY CARROLL & CHERI GREGORY

Go back to the list of seed senders that you made in response to the first question today. How can you follow their example? By doing so, how would you honor God and your seed senders?

At the end of the chapter, how did the summary "Live life as a vibrant seed sender" hit you? Do you believe you can? Why or why not?

A BREATH OF FRESH AIR

:

If you'd like to hear more related to this topic, you can listen to Episode #60 of

Grit 'n' Grace "How to Embrace the Unexpected Choice" at

https://gritngracegirls.com/episode60/

© AMY CARROLL & CHERI GREGORY

Day 2:

_____READ CHAPTER 16

_____COMPLETE "NOW BREATHE" AT THE END OF THE CHAPTER

_____ANSWER THE QUESTIONS

My "Now Breathe" Notes:

© AMY CARROLL & CHERI GREGORY

Review the parable of the talents in Matthew 25:14-18. If you could hone one gift or talent, what would it be?

How would it change your life to embrace the gift of focus in this one area?

Remember back. When you let go of a dead dream in the past, what grew in its place? Thank God for that growth, and let it build your faith for future letting go.

How does this chapter change your perspective on how God "gives and takes away"?

© AMY CARROLL & CHERI GREGORY

At the end of the chapter, how did the summary "Live open to God's direction and redirection" hit you? Do you believe you can? Why or why not?

A BREATH OF FRESH AIR

If you'd like to hear more about this topic, download these

"Growing Into a Calling" PDFs at Amy's website:

https://amycarroll.org/wp-content/uploads/2013/11/Growing-Into-A-Calling-Part-1.pdf

https://amycarroll.org/wp-content/uploads/2013/11/Growing-Into-A-Calling-Part-2.pdf

© AMY CARROLL & CHERI GREGORY

Day 3:

_____Read chapter 17

_____Complete "Now Breathe" at the end of the chapter

_____Answer the questions

My "Now Breathe" Notes:

© Amy Carroll & Cheri Gregory

Review the story of the woman freed from a spirit in Luke 13:10-17. Name one thing that God has freed you from.

What is the first thing that comes to mind when you hear "God is my refuge"?

How could allowing God to be your refuge free you to meet a need with your name on it?

Reread the story about Cheri sending a copy of *Tear Soup* to a grieving woman. Who have you avoided ministering to because you thought *She needs anyone but me* or feared doing/saying the wrong thing? This week, do the thing that has been on your heart even if your head tells you, "That won't help."

© AMY CARROLL & CHERI GREGORY

At the end of the chapter, how did the summary "Live free to meet the need with your name on it" hit you? Do you believe you can? Why or why not?

A BREATH OF FRESH AIR

If you'd like to hear more about this topic, listen to episode #34 of Grit 'n' Grace. You can find "Together in the Wait—Building Care, Compassion, and Community in the Waiting" at

https://gritngracegirls.com/episode34

© Amy Carroll & Cheri Gregory

Day 4:

_____READ CHAPTER 18

_____COMPLETE "NOW BREATHE" AT THE END OF THE CHAPTER

_____ANSWER THE QUESTIONS

My "Now Breathe" Notes:

© AMY CARROLL & CHERI GREGORY

This week, read Jesus' prayer from John 17 at least once. Try reading it out loud. What does it reveal about his love for you?

What does John 17 reveal about His love for those you care about?

Who has God gifted you to care for—who do you consider "His assignment"? Are you prioritizing those people?

Amy says, "Loving God. Loving people. That's the recipe for a life that counts." As you grow in living out this truth, how will it help you to live the "seize the yay" life?

© AMY CARROLL & CHERI GREGORY

At the end of the chapter, how did the summary "Live in celebration of God's fullest life in you" hit you? Do you believe you can? Why or why not?

A BREATH OF FRESH AIR

If you'd like to hear more related to this topic, you can listen to Episode #75 of

Grit 'n' Grace "Finding New Ways to Be Better Together" ant

https://gritngracegirls.com/episode75

© AMY CARROLL & CHERI GREGORY

Day 5:

_____THE BREATHING SPACE

Revisit Cheri's favorite verse again, Psalm 18:19, "He [God] brought me out into a spacious place; he rescued me because he delighted in me." (NIV)

We want you to feel the spaciousness in this book and its process. It's definitely not our intent to smother you with One More Thing! Our last day will be set aside to simply reflect and process. Please use this time to allow the change that God is doing to soak deep into your soul.

From the changes you experienced as you read Exhale and did the study, how will you: Glorify God?

Fulfill the longings of your heart?

Meet the needs of your people?

© AMY CARROLL & CHERI GREGORY

List the ways that you feel more equipped to live your one life well.

Write three main points from this study that you want to stick in your heart and mind as you move back into everyday life.

Now, take time to pray. Thank God for what He's done, and ask Him to continue the unfinished work. Tell Him that you want the lessons that you've learned in this study to be sealed in your heart.

exhale

© AMY CARROLL & CHERI GREGORY

Notes:

© Amy Carroll & Cheri Gregory

GROUP GATHERING #6

Seed Sender Celebration

SUPPLIES NEEDED:

Small plastic cups, potting soil, seeds (pick the kind that delights your heart-- herbs, flowers…), any party supplies and food that delight your heart

10 MINUTES-- ACTIVITY:

As women come in, have them plant their seed as a reminder to be a seed sender. Discuss how the idea of being a seed sender impacts them.

15-20 MINUTES– VIDEO TEACHING #6:

You can access all of them at ExhaleBook.com/Study

20-25 MINUTES– DISCUSSION:

During this time, along with any other questions from the week, have women share how they feel better equipped to fulfill the desires of their hearts, love their people well, and glorify God.

10 MINUTES– SMALL GROUP PRAYER:

Ask participants to share a quick praise for what God has done in them through the study. Have an ending prayer time filled with praise and thanksgiving. We give you permission to get loud and rowdy.

CELEBRATE! TAKE PHOTOS, AND POST THEM ON SOCIAL MEDIA WITH

#EXHALEBOOK #SEIZETHEYAY #SEEDSENDERS.

© AMY CARROLL & CHERI GREGORY

Notes:

© Amy Carroll & Cheri Gregory

This Doesn't Have to Be Good-Bye

It has been our great delight to write *Exhale* and the discussion guides for you. As we've poured over every word again and again to get it just right for you, we've imagined you reading and learning and growing, just like we did as we wrote. We hope you feel the deep love we've developed for you!

The journey doesn't have to end here. There are ways to keep in touch with us.

Read on to learn about our other resources as well as how you can stay connected.

Amy Carroll

Amy Carroll loves connecting a community through cultivating tender hearts and strong voices. There's nothing that delights her heart more than moving through life with Jesus and her tribe of tender-spoken women.

Amy is the author of *Breaking Up with Perfect*, a member of the Proverbs 31 Ministries speaker and writer teams and co-host of the *Grit 'n' Grace* podcast.

As a consummate southern girl, Amy loves words that shape a great story and a challenging idea. She writes monthly devotions for *Encouragement for Today*, weekly blog posts at amycarroll.org and revels in podcast conversations with Cheri Gregory at gritngracegirls.com.

Amy also loves to help other speakers give birth to their messages. She is the founder and speaker coach of Next Step Coaching Services which provides one-on-one training for Christian speakers and writers.

Amy's other book: *Breaking Up with Perfect*

Her website and blog: amycarroll.org

Her speaker coaching services: nextstepcoachingservices.com

Facebook: @amydohmcarroll

Instagram: @amydohmcarroll

To inquire about having Amy speak for your next event, visit proverbs31.org/speakers or call the Proverbs 31 Ministries office at 1-877-731-4663.

CHERI GREGORY

Through scripture and storytelling, Cheri loves sharing experiences that connect to women's frustrations, fears, and failures, giving them hope that they are not alone—someone gets them.

As paradigm-shifter, Cheri believes that "how-to" works best in partnership with "heart-to." She loves engaging in conversations that lead to transformations via Skype interviews with Amy and *Grit 'n' Grace* podcast guests.

Cheri is the co-author, with Kathi Lipp, of *You Don't Have to Try So Hard* and *Overwhelmed*; the co-host of the Grit 'n' Grace podcast; and the co-leader of Sensitive and Strong: the place for the HSP woman to find Community. She also serves as the curriculum director and alumni coordinator for the LEVERAGE Speaker Conference.

Cheri also loves to help speakers move their message from the stage to the page. Through Write Beside You, she offers one-on-one coaching and online eCourses for Christian speakers and writers.

Cheri's other books, co-authored with Kathi Lipp: *You Don't Have to Try So Hard* and

Overwhelmed

Her websites: CheriGregory.com and SensitiveAndStrong.com

Her writer coaching services: WriteBesideYou.com

Facebook: @Cheri.Gregory.Author

Instagram: @cheri_gregory

To inquire about having Cheri speak for your next event, visit her website at CheriGregory.com/contact or email Info@CheriGregory.com

Book a Speaking Event

WE ESPECIALLY ADORE SPEAKING TOGETHER!

INVITE US TO YOUR EVENT TODAY TO DO A
GRIT 'N' GRACE OR EXHALE CONFERENCE.
EMAIL: AMYNCHERI@GRITNGRACEGIRLS.COM

© AMY CARROLL & CHERI GREGORY

Thank You

A huge thank you to our Grit 'n' Grace interns who helped write the content for this group study: Iris Bryant, Jenn Bryant, Jeanette Hanscomb, Rachel Latham, Melissa McLamb, Chris Moss, Vicki Stone, and Lori Young.

© Amy Carroll & Cheri Gregory

MOVE FROM RUNNING-ON-EMPTY TO SPENT-AND-CONTENT.

Exhale, the transforming book for the woman suffocating under the pressure of being all things to all people, is changing lives. This companion, a six-week group study, is designed to take the life-changing lessons from the book to an even deeper level, creating change that sticks through group discussion and support.

In this study, rather than adding more to your to-do list, Amy Carroll and Cheri Gregory show you how to

- **Lose** the ill-fitting roles you've been trying to fill so that you can be lighter and freer

- **Love** your truest, God-created self with all your glorious gifts instead of trying to shove yourself into a mold

- **Live** your one and only life in a way that you know truly matters

Combining Scripture, thought-provoking questions and time to inhale the lesson of *Exhale,* the group study will empower you and your friends to walk through a process that releases you from the things that have created unbearable pressure. Then you'll be able to live the combination we all long for: fulfilling the desires of your heart, loving your people well, *and* bringing glory to God.

AMY CARROLL is a member of the speaker and writer teams for Proverbs 31 Ministries. She's the author of *Breaking Up with Perfect* and a co-host for the podcast *Grit 'n' Grace.* Amy and her husband live in Holly Springs, North Carolina. Find out more at www.amycarroll.org

CHERI GREGORY is a frequent speaker and the coauthor, with Kathi Lipp, of *You Don't Have to Try So Hard* and *Overwhelmed.* She's also a contributor to the *(in)courage Devotional Bible.* She lives with her family on the central California coast. Learn more at www.cherigregory.com

10909550R00057

Made in the USA
Monee, IL
03 September 2019